Holiday Cooking for Kids!

HALLOWEEN
Sweets and Treats

By Ruth Owen

WINDMILL
BOOKS ™

New York

Published in 2013 by Windmill Books, An Imprint of Rosen Publishing
29 East 21st Street, New York, NY 10010

First Edition

Produced for Windmill by Ruby Tuesday Books Ltd
Editor for Ruby Tuesday Books Ltd: Mark J. Sachner
US Editor: Sara Antill
Designers: Trudi Webb and Emma Randall

Photo Credits:
Cover, 1, 3, 4–5, 6–7, 8, 9 (top), 10, 11 (top), 11 (center), 11 (bottom left), 12–13, 14–15, 16–17, 18–19, 20–21, 22–23, 24–25, 26–27, 28–29, 30, 31 (top) © Shutterstock; 9 (bottom right), 11 (bottom right), 31 (bottom) © Ruby Tuesday Books Ltd.

Library of Congress Cataloging-in-Publication Data

Owen, Ruth, 1967–
  Halloween sweets and treats / by Ruth Owen.
      p. cm. — (Holiday cooking for kids!)
  Includes index.
  ISBN 978-1-4488-8079-9 (library binding) — ISBN 978-1-4488-8126-0 (pbk.) — ISBN 978-1-4488-8132-1 (6-pack)
  1. Halloween cooking—Juvenile literature. 2. Desserts—Juvenile literature. I. Title.
  TX739.2.H34.O95 2013
   641.5'68—dc23

                            2012009216

Manufactured in the United States of America

CPSIA Compliance Information: Batch # B3S12WM: For Further Information contact Windmill Books, New York, New York at 1-866-478-0556

Contents

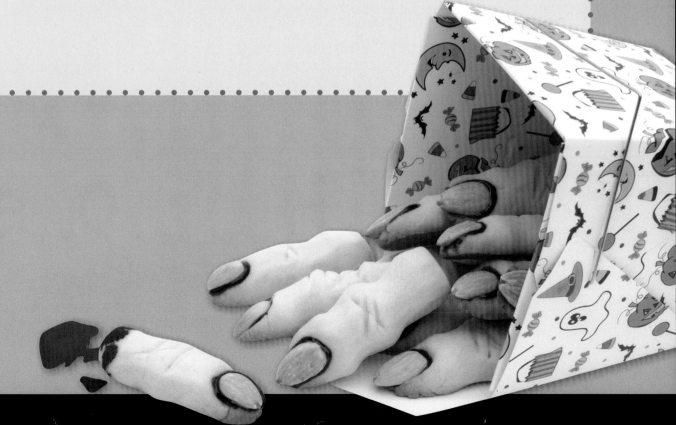

Hundreds of years ago, tribal groups in parts of Europe, including present-day Britain, Ireland, and France, celebrated their New Year on November 1. This made October 31, the date of our present-day Halloween, their New Year's Eve and a night of celebration.

Ancient people also believed that on October 31, the human world and the **spirit** world were at their closest. On this night, it was believed that spirits of the dead would return to Earth.

If people went out at night, they dressed in ways intended to trick the spirits who were roaming around. By disguising themselves with masks and costumes, people hoped ghosts would think they were spirits and not living human beings.

Today, people still dress up on October 31. We also hand out sweets and other foods to satisfy the appetites of wandering spirits and humans alike!

HAPPY HALLOWEEN

The recipes in this book will give you many ways to conjure up more finger-licking Halloween fun!

Before you start cooking, check out all the tips and information on the following pages.

Get Ready to Cook

- Wash your hands using soap and hot water. This will help to keep bacteria away from your food.
- Make sure the kitchen countertop and all your equipment is clean.
- Read the recipe carefully before you start cooking. If you don't understand a step, ask an adult to help you.
- Gather all the ingredients and equipment you will need.

Safety First!

It's very, very important to have an adult around whenever you do any of the following tasks in the kitchen:

1. Operating machinery or turning on kitchen appliances such as a mixer, food processor, blender, stovetop burners, or the oven.

2. Using sharp utensils, such as knives, can openers, or vegetable peelers.

3. Working with hot pots, pans, or cookie sheets.

Food processor

Mixing bowl

Saucepan

Rolling pin

Cutting board

Knife

Frying pan

Sieve

Wooden spoon

You will need these kitchen utensils to make the recipes in this book.

Spatula

Pastry brush

Grater

Electric hand mixer

Oven mitt

Baking pan

Cupcake pan

Cookie sheet

Measuring Counts!

Measure your ingredients carefully. If you get a measurement wrong, it could affect how successful your dish turns out to be. Measuring cups and spoons are two of the most important pieces of equipment in a kitchen.

Measuring cup

Measuring Cups

Measuring cups are used to measure the volume, or amount, of liquid or dry ingredients. Measuring cups usually hold from 1 cup to 4 cups. If you have a 1-cup measuring cup, that should be fine for all the recipes in this book. Measuring cups have markings on them that show how many cups or parts of a cup you are measuring.

Measuring Spoons

Like measuring cups, measuring spoons are used to measure the volume of liquid or dry ingredients, only in smaller amounts. Measuring spoons come in sets with different spoons for teaspoons, tablespoons, and smaller parts.

Measuring spoons

Cooking Techniques

Here are some tasks that anyone who is following directions for cooking should be sure to understand.

Bringing to a boil

Heating a liquid or mixture in a saucepan on the stovetop until it is bubbling.

Simmering

First bringing a liquid or mixture to a boil, and then turning down the heat so it's just at or below the boiling point and the bubbling has nearly stopped.

Preheating

Heating the oven until it has reached the temperature required for the recipe.

All of these tasks require the use of heat, so you should be absolutely sure to have an adult around when you do them.

Monster Caramel Apples

If you want to make a delicious Halloween treat that's sweet and horribly good for you, caramel apples is the way to go.

Fall is the time of year when apples are harvested from **orchards**. So whether you buy the apples from a store or visit an apple farm and pick your own, this recipe is a great way to enjoy fresh, crunchy apples!

Treats With Tricks

Eating apple peels is a great way to get antioxidants into your body. Antioxidants are substances that help to keep our bodies healthy. Apple peels contain lots of **fiber**, too. Fiber is the stuff that keeps your digestive system working!

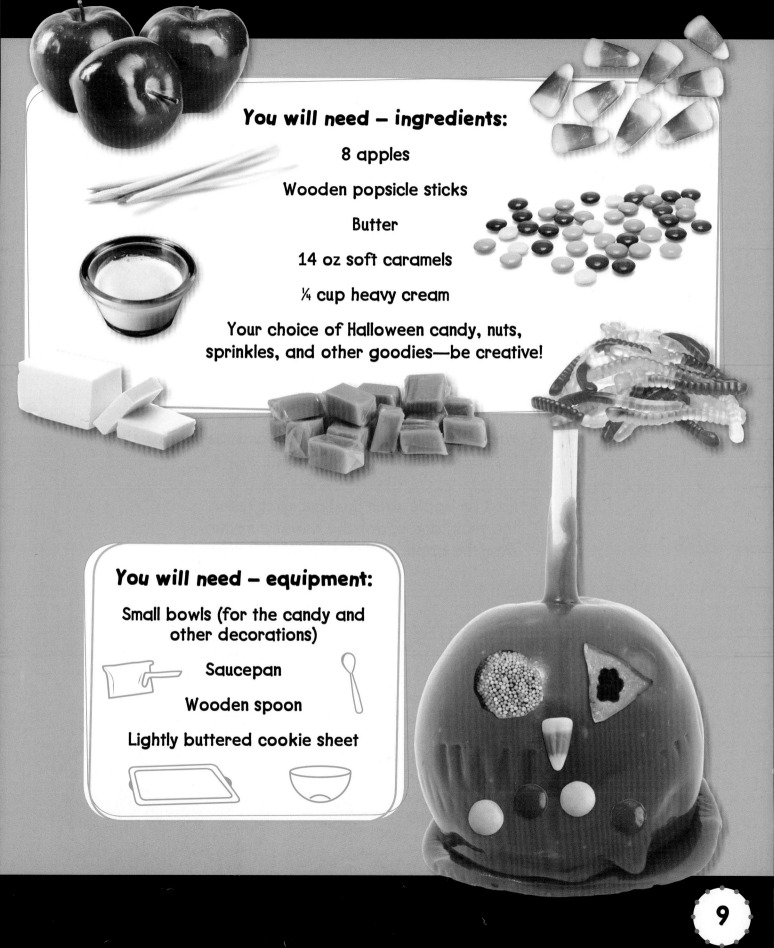

You will need – ingredients:

8 apples

Wooden popsicle sticks

Butter

14 oz soft caramels

¼ cup heavy cream

Your choice of Halloween candy, nuts, sprinkles, and other goodies—be creative!

You will need – equipment:

Small bowls (for the candy and other decorations)

Saucepan

Wooden spoon

Lightly buttered cookie sheet

Step-by-Step:

Remember to ask an adult for help when you are using the stove.

1. Put the candy, sprinkles, and other delicious decorations into small individual bowls.

2. Push a stick into each apple at the stem end.

3. Unwrap the caramels and put them into the saucepan with the cream. Heat the caramels and cream on a low to medium heat.

4. As the caramels melt into the cream, stir the mixture using the wooden spoon.

5. When the caramels have melted and the mixture is smooth, remove from the heat.

6. Hold an apple over the saucepan (using the stick) and spoon the caramel mixture over the apple until it is completely coated.

TIP:
If the caramel mixture starts to get stiff, put the saucepan back over a low heat and stir until the mixture becomes runny again.

Step-by-Step:

7. Now comes the really fun part! Decorate the caramel apples by pressing candy into the caramel. You can dip the apples into decorations, such as sprinkles, to completely cover them. You can also use the candy to make horrible Halloween monster faces!

8. Put the caramel apples on the buttered cookie sheet to cool off for about 10 minutes.

Roasted Jack-o'-Lantern Pumpkin Seeds

In ancient Ireland, people carved out turnips and potatoes and placed candles inside to scare away evil spirits at Halloween. When European settlers came to America, Native Americans introduced them to pumpkins. Today, we use pumpkins to create the fun and scary-looking faces that we know as jack-o'-lanterns. Here's something you can do with the seeds that are left over from carving pumpkins to make jack-o'-lanterns. Roasted and salted, pumpkin seeds make a delicious, nutritious snack!

You will need – ingredients:

Pumpkin (or pumpkins) for carving jack-o'-lanterns

2 cups pumpkin seeds
(from fresh pumpkins)

1 tablespoon vegetable oil

1 tablespoon butter (or margarine), softened

1–2 teaspoons salt

You will need – equipment:

Narrow-bladed knife (use with adult supervision)

Large tablespoon

Medium bowl

Wooden spoon

Baking pan

Potholder or oven mitt for handling baking pan

Step-by-Step:

Remember to ask an adult for help when you are using the knife and stove.

1. Have an adult help you cut the pumpkins to make the jack-o'-lanterns. Be sure that each pumpkin has a hole cut in it big enough to reach in and clean out the seeds!

2. Preheat oven to 225°F (100°C).

3. Use the large tablespoon to scoop out all the seeds and the stringy material.

4. Separate the seeds from the stringy material. Don't bother washing off the seeds, as any remaining bits and pieces of "flesh" on them will add to the flavor when the seeds are roasted.

5. In the bowl, mix the seeds with the oil, butter, and salt.

6. Spread the seeds on the baking pan.

7. With an adult supervising, bake the seeds until they are crisp and golden, for about an hour. Stir the seeds on the sheet every 10 to 15 minutes so they don't burn on the pan.

8. When the seeds are done, remove the pan from the oven and slide the seeds off into a bowl for serving them. When they have cooled, start snacking!

Halloween Cookies

Baking and decorating cookies is great fun. This recipe gives you a basic and easy-to-make cookie **dough** to get you started. Then it's up to you how creative or how horrific you get with your decorations. You can make simple, but delicious, round cookies covered with Halloween candy or sprinkles. Why not get into the Halloween spirit, however, and make some gruesome headless and legless cookie people?

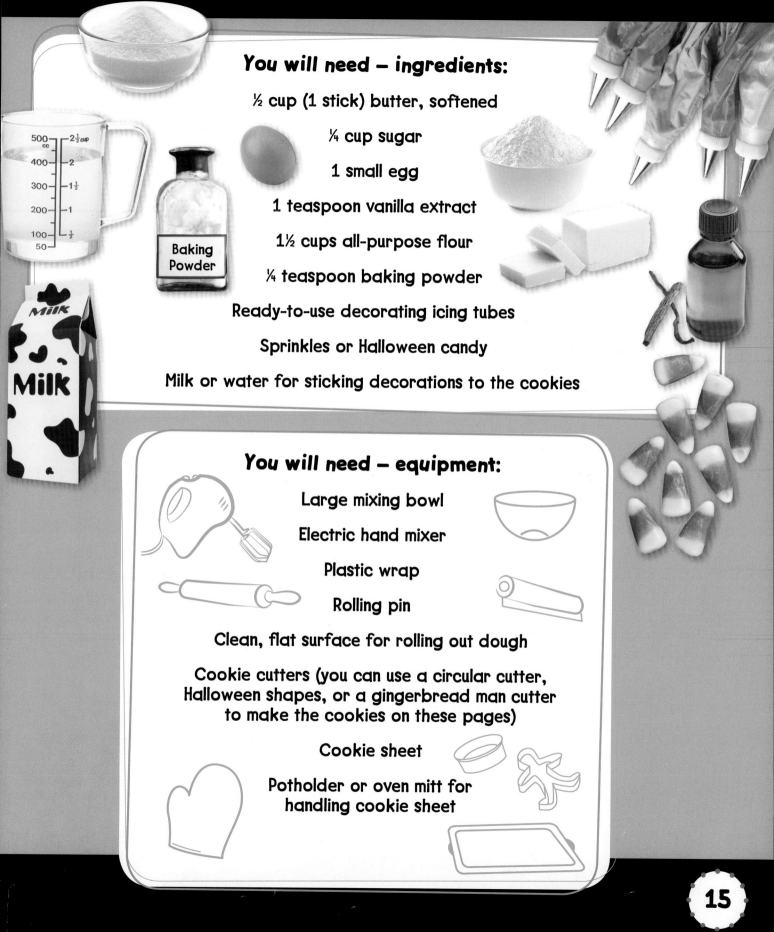

You will need – ingredients:

½ cup (1 stick) butter, softened

¼ cup sugar

1 small egg

1 teaspoon vanilla extract

1½ cups all-purpose flour

¼ teaspoon baking powder

Ready-to-use decorating icing tubes

Sprinkles or Halloween candy

Milk or water for sticking decorations to the cookies

You will need – equipment:

Large mixing bowl

Electric hand mixer

Plastic wrap

Rolling pin

Clean, flat surface for rolling out dough

Cookie cutters (you can use a circular cutter,
Halloween shapes, or a gingerbread man cutter
to make the cookies on these pages)

Cookie sheet

Potholder or oven mitt for
handling cookie sheet

Remember to ask an adult for help when you are using the electric hand mixer and oven.

Step-by-Step:

Steps 1 to 3 below make a basic cookie dough. You can use the same recipe to make the Crunchy Witch's Fingers on pages 18–19.

1. Using the electric mixer, beat the butter and sugar together until creamy, then add the egg and vanilla extract and beat until well blended.

2. Gradually add the flour and baking powder, and beat until it's just blended.

3. Shape the dough into a ball, wrap in plastic wrap, and cool in the refrigerator for an hour or in the freezer for 30 minutes.

4. Ask an adult to help you preheat the oven to 350°F (175°C).

5. Place the chilled dough on a flat, lightly floured surface and roll out until it's about ¼ inch (0.6 cm) thick

6. Now it's time to get creative! To make round decorated cookies, use the circular cookie cutter. You can press Halloween candy into the tops of the cookies. To decorate with sprinkles, smear a little water or milk over the top of the cookies (to act like glue), and then toss the sprinkles over the cookies. (You can also make a sugary "glue" to stick on your decorations. See the recipe on pages 18–19.)

Step-by-Step:

7. Make spooky shapes using Halloween cookie cutters.

8. To make the headless and legless cookie people, use a gingerbread man cookie cutter. You can either chop off their body parts now, or snap them off when the cookies are baked!

9. Place the cookies 1 inch (2.5 cm) apart on the cookie sheet and bake in the preheated oven for 10–12 minutes, or until lightly browned. Take out to cool.

10. When the ready-decorated cookies are cool, they're ready to eat.

11. When the Halloween shapes or headless people have cooled, have fun decorating them with the icing. Be as gruesome as you like!

Crunchy Witch's Fingers

These witch's fingers look horrifying, but they taste great! You can use the cookie dough recipe from pages 16–17 to make a batch of crunchy fingers for your Halloween party.

You will need – ingredients:

½ cup (1 stick) butter, softened

¼ cup sugar

1 small egg

1 teaspoon vanilla extract

1½ cups all-purpose flour

¼ teaspoon baking powder

½ cup whole or sliced almonds

¼ cup confectioners (powdered) sugar

1 teaspoon water

You will need – equipment:

Large mixing bowl

Small bowl

Electric hand mixer

Plastic wrap

Cookie sheet

Potholder or oven mitt for handling cookie sheet

Butter knife

Small spoon (for stirring sugar glue)

Step-by-Step:

1. Follow steps 1 to 3 on page 16 to make the basic cookie dough.

2. Ask an adult to help you preheat the oven to 350°F (175°C).

3. Take a lump of dough (about a heaping tablespoon) and with your hands roll it into a finger shape.

4. Place each finger about 1 inch (2.5 cm) apart on the cookie sheet. Use a butter knife to make knuckle marks on the finger cookies and flatten one end to make a place for the fingernail.

5. Bake the cookies in the preheated oven for about 12-15 minutes, or until they look slightly golden. Remove from the oven and allow to cool.

6. To make the sugar glue, mix some powdered sugar and water together in the small bowl to make a paste.

7. Stick the almonds to the ends of the fingers using a little blob of sugar glue under each almond. Then allow the glue to dry for about 30 minutes. Get crunching!

Remember to ask an adult for help when you are using the electric hand mixer and oven.

TIP:
For added color, glue on the fingernails using red or brown ready-to-use decorating icing, and let it ooze out from under the almond. You can also dip the cut-off ends of the fingers in red jam to make them look bloody!

19

Perfect Pumpkin Soup

Native people have been growing pumpkins for over 5,000 years, which makes the pumpkin a truly all-American food! Today, about 99 percent of all pumpkins grown in North America are sold at Halloween, and we all know the main reason people buy them is to carve jack-o'-lanterns! But pumpkins are also terrific for making good food. Here is a recipe for a pumpkin soup that is warm, hearty, and so satisfying that it'll tickle the taste buds of returning trick or treaters!

You will need – ingredients:

These quantities make six small servings of soup

3 (15-ounce) cans pureed pumpkin

1 tablespoon minced or finely chopped garlic

1 large sweet onion, chopped

6 carrots, finely chopped or grated

2 stalks (not 2 bunches!) celery, chopped

3 tablespoons melted butter (or margarine)

1 pint (16 ounces) half-and-half

2 teaspoons dried thyme

½ teaspoon salt

Dash ($\frac{1}{8}$ teaspoon) pepper

4 tablespoons dried parsley or chopped fresh parsley

Roasted pumpkin seeds for serving (optional; see recipe on page 12)

You will need – equipment:

Fork or potato masher

Knife for chopping

Grater (if desired for carrots)

Medium bowl

Saucepan

Wooden spoon for stirring

Potholder or oven mitt for handling hot saucepan

Step-by-Step:

Remember to ask an adult for help when you are using the knife and stove.

1. In a bowl, use a fork or potato masher to be sure that the pumpkin is mashed up.

2. Heat and melt the butter in the saucepan.

3. Add onion, celery, and carrots to saucepan, allowing them to fry lightly until tender. Stir every few seconds to keep them from burning.

4. Add the garlic, thyme, salt, pepper, and parsley into the saucepan, and stir to mix all the ingredients.

5. Add the pumpkin, stirring so that all the ingredients are mixed thoroughly.

6. Add the half-and-half and stir into rest of soup mixture.

7. With an adult supervising, bring mixture to a boil and quickly reduce heat so the soup will simmer.

8. Cover and let simmer for at least 10 minutes, stirring occasionally.

9. Serve hot and sprinkle with roasted pumpkin seeds to add a little salty crunch!

Treats With Tricks

Pumpkins are a type of fruit and belong to the same family as squash and melons. Cucumbers and zucchini are also varieties of squash, and they are therefore related to pumpkins as well. Like pumpkins, cukes and zukes are often thought of as vegetables. That's because they are heated and mixed with other ingredients in much the same way that vegetables are, and they are served in meals as vegetable dishes.

Eyeball Cupcakes

The only "scary" thing about these **edible** eyeballs will be trying to figure out what to do with them. Should you place them over your eyes and make your friends laugh, or bite into them and give your taste buds a treat! If you're serving these creepy cupcakes at a Halloween party, be sure to make enough. Your **ghoulish** guests will want one for each eye!

You will need – ingredients:

These quantities will make about 10 to 12 cupcakes

To make the cupcakes:

1 cup sugar

½ cup butter, softened

2 eggs

2 teaspoons vanilla extract

1½ cups all-purpose flour

1¾ teaspoons baking powder

½ cup milk

Jelly beans, round gumdrops, ring-shaped gummy candies and fruit snacks, and any other round candies that can be used to decorate the eyeballs

Ready-to-use decorating icing tubes (red and black, but also any other colors you might want to use)

To make the frosting:

8 ounce (226 g) package of cream cheese, softened

¼ cup butter, softened

1 teaspoon vanilla extract

16 ounce (453 g) package of confectioners' (powdered) sugar, sifted

You will need – equipment:

Cupcake pan

Paper cupcake liners

Large mixing bowl

Wooden spoon

Sieve for sifting flour

Medium mixing bowl

Electric hand mixer

Toothpick

Potholder or oven mitt for handling cupcake pan

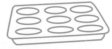

Step-by-Step:

To make the cupcakes:

1. Line the cupcake pan with the paper cupcake liners.

2. In the large mixing bowl, use the electric mixer to mix together the sugar and butter.

3. One at a time, beat the eggs into the sugar and butter mixture, then stir in the vanilla extract.

4. In the medium bowl, sift together the flour and baking powder.

5. Add the flour mixture to the creamy mixture and mix thoroughly.

6. Add the milk, stirring until the batter is smooth.

7. Ask an adult to help you preheat the oven to 350°F (175°C).

8. Pour the batter into the paper cupcake liners so that each liner is about ²/₃ full.

9. Bake for 20–25 minutes, until the cupcakes are light brown. Test to see if they're done by sticking a toothpick into the center of a cupcake. If it comes out clean, your cupcakes are ready to take out of the oven!

Step-by-Step:

10. When the cupcakes have cooled, spread their tops with frosting (see recipe below) to create the "whites" of the eyes. Add round or circle-shaped candies to create the pupils. Then apply ready-to-use red icing to make the eyes look bloodshot. You can also use black icing to create eyeliner, eyelashes, or anything else to make your cupcake eyeballs look as creepy as you like, or just to give them that special spooky stare!

To make the frosting:

1. Stir together the cream cheese, butter, and vanilla extract in the medium bowl and use the electric mixer to beat them together until well blended.

2. Gradually beat in the sugar so it blends with the creamy mixture.

Haunted Black Bean and Corn Dip

From hayrides to candy corn, to multicolored Indian corn, to scaring ourselves by getting lost in corn mazes, corn has long been associated with fall and Halloween. Most corn is harvested in the late summer and fall and, along with pumpkins, is a truly American food. Its roots go back to Native people developing it for food and trade throughout Latin America and into North America for thousands of years before Europeans even knew there was such a thing as corn! So what could be a more perfect, healthy Halloween dish than a dip made out of corn and black beans? And to top it off, corn chips or homemade tortilla chips with spooky Halloween shapes!

You will need – ingredients:

To make the dip:

1 cup frozen corn kernels

1 teaspoon vegetable or olive oil

1½ cups cooked black beans, drained

2 to 4 tablespoons salsa (available in jars with different degrees of spiciness)

2 tablespoons water or enough for blending

1 tablespoon freshly squeezed lime juice

½ teaspoon hot sauce

¼ to ½ teaspoon ground cumin

½ teaspoon salt

2 tablespoons fresh basil leaves, chopped small enough to fit tightly into measuring spoon

¼ cup chopped red pepper

Carrot and celery sticks

To make the tortilla chips:

9 flour or corn tortillas about 7 inches (18 cm) across

2¼ teaspoons taco or chili seasoning

Vegetable or olive oil (enough to brush onto the chips)

You will need – equipment:

Wooden spoon

Large and medium mixing bowls

Food processor or blender

Frying pan

Cookie cutters in ghost or other Halloween shapes

Pastry brush

Cookie sheet

Spatula

Potholder or oven mitt for handling cookie sheet

Step-by-Step:

To make the dip:

1. Combine the oil and corn in the frying pan and heat, stirring often, until the corn is slightly browned.

2. Remove frying pan from heat and transfer corn to medium bowl to cool.

3. In the large mixing bowl, stir together black beans, salsa, lime juice, hot sauce, and cumin.

4. Blend the mixture in the food processor. You can make the mixture as chunky or smooth as you like. If you prefer the smoother mixture, you can add water to make it as thick or thin as you like.

5. Add salt to the blended mixture to suit your taste.

6. Spoon the mixture out of the food processor and into the large bowl.

7. Stir in the corn and basil.

8. Serve topped with chopped red pepper. Stick tortilla chips in the dip or place on the side, along with carrot and celery sticks.

Step-by-step:

To make the tortilla chips:

1. Cut Halloween shapes out of tortillas with cookie cutters.

2. Ask an adult to help you preheat the oven to 350°F (175°C).

3. Place the tortilla cutouts on the cookie sheet.

4. Using a pastry brush, spread a small amount of oil on each side of the cutouts.

5. Use your fingers to lightly sprinkle taco or chili seasoning on each side of the cutouts.

6. Bake in the preheated oven for 8–10 minutes, or until the edges just begin to brown. Remove from oven and allow to cool.

7. Slide the tortilla chips off the cookie sheet and enjoy the blend of fresh and savory flavors as your chips plunge into the dip!

Glossary

dough (DOH) A thick mixture of flour and water, used for making such baked products as bread and cookies.

edible (EH-deh-bul) Good enough, or fit, to be eaten.

fiber (FY-ber) A substance found in celery, cereals, and other plants that the human body can't break down and that helps move food through our digestive systems.

ghoulish (GOO-lish) Grisly or horrific; the original meaning of "ghoul" had to do with legendary monsters that ate dead flesh

orchard (OR-cherd) A farm that grows fruit, or the area on a farm where fruit trees are planted.

spirit (SPIR-ut) The part of human beings that is associated with the soul or a similar nonphysical state; often used to describe a ghost or some other presence after death.

Index

Websites

For web resources related to the subject of this book, go to: www.windmillbooks.com/weblinks and select this book's title.